ANCIENT EGYPTIAN CULTURE

ANCIENT EGYPTIAN CULTURE

CHARTWELL
BOOKS, INC.

Published by Chartwell Books
A Division of Book Sales Inc.
114 Northfield Avenue
Edison, New Jersey 08837
USA

0-7858-0996-1

This book is produced by
Quantum Books Ltd
6 Blundell Street
London N7 9BH

Project Manager: Rebecca Kingsley
Project Editor: Judith Millidge
Designer: Wayne Humphries
Editor: Sarah Halliwell

The material in this publication previously appeared in
Egyptology, *Pyramids* & *Ancient Egyptians*

QUMAEC
Set in Times
Reproduced in Singapore by United Graphic Ltd
Printed in Singapore by Star Standard Industries (Pte) Ltd

CONTENTS

INTRODUCTION

The Ancient Egyptian civilization lasted for many centuries, from around 3000-300 B.C. During that time, the Egyptians created massive buildings and elegant works of art. They invented systems of writing, measuring, and counting. They developed a strong, centralized government. Egyptian designs and technological achievements were admired – and sometimes copied – in many countries of the ancient world. And their mysterious, complicated religious beliefs still fascinate scholars and writers today.

Yet what do we know of this remote world of beautiful but obscure hieroglyphics and colorful tomb paintings? Western civilization is still young after 2000 years compared with the 3000-year-old civilization of the Ancient Egyptians, which remained just an awe-inspiring mystery until serious study of the people and its culture began in the last 200 years.

The study of Ancient Egypt has been greatly aided by the survival of a vast quantity of artifacts. Many of these have survived because of the Egyptian belief in an afterlife which would be a magnificent extension of the earthly life. Kings and merchants surrounded themselves both with treasures and more mundane objects that would help and comfort them in the afterlife.

The earliest Egyptians were nomads, wandering in search of food and water. But by around 2900 B.C., the time of the first recorded Egyptian ruling family, they had been settled in villages along the banks of the Nile for hundreds, perhaps thousands, of years. The kingdom of Ancient Egypt grew up along the banks of the River Nile in North Africa. It was well-positioned for contact with both Mediterranean and Middle Eastern early civilizations. The River Nile provided a long strip of fertile land which was perfect for growing crops. Including the Delta, it covered about 34,000 square kilometers. The Ancient Egyptians settled on the river's banks around 3000 B.C. and formed one of the most sophisticated early civilizations.

From these simple beginnings, the Egyptian state grew very strong. Egyptian kings – pharaohs – ruled a large empire. They fought and conquered far-away peoples, in present-day Syria, Libya, and Iraq. And they traded with merchants from other ancient civilizations, such as the Lebanese and the Greeks, who lived around the Mediterranean Sea.

Most Egyptian buildings, and many works of art, are decorated with inscriptions – lines of picture-writing called hieroglyphics carved into their hard-stone surface. Because stone is so tough, and lasts so long, these inscriptions can still be read even after many centuries have passed. Often they are a record of a great achievement, like building a temple or winning a war. The Egyptians hoped that these messages in stone would last for ever. We can also learn about the Egyptians from travellers, such as the Greek writer

Opposite below left: A Servant from the pharaoh's palace carring food to offer the Gods.

Below: Fowling in the marshes. Large areas of the marshland around the Nile were carefully preserved for fishing, which was a prosperous occupation for the Ancient Egyptians. From a Theban tomb painting, c.1400 B.C.

Herodotus, who visited the country around 500 B.C. These travel-writings are often very useful, although we cannot believe everything they say: Herodotus, for example, included scandalous and far-fetched stories merely to entertain his readers.

Even though the Ancient Egyptian people lived so long ago, we can still find out about their lifestyles, customs and beliefs. Our information comes from different kinds of evidence – buildings, statues, tombs, inscriptions, and many smaller objects – that have survived from ancient times. Thanks to Egypt's warm, dry, desert climate, many monuments have survived remarkably well. These tombs and temples were decorated with carvings, paintings, and statues. Some show everyday activities, others show religious scenes. They all tell us something about the way people lived – how they fought and farmed, went hunting, said their prayers, or simply enjoyed themselves. They also help us to discover what the Egyptians looked like, what they ate, and what clothes they wore – their culture.

THE STUDY OF ANCIENT EGYPT

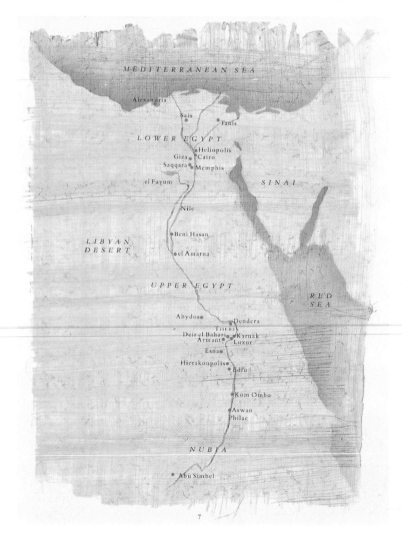

MEDITERRANEAN SEA

Alexandria

Sais
Tanis

LOWER EGYPT

Heliopolis
Giza • Cairo
Saqqara • Memphis

el Fayum

SINAI

Nile

Beni Hasan

LIBYAN
DESERT

el Amarna

UPPER EGYPT

RED
SEA

Abydos

Dendera
THEBES
Deir el Bahari • Karnak
Armant • Luxor
Esna
Hierakonpolis • Edfu

Kom Ombo

Aswan
Philae

NUBIA

Abu Simbel

7

Although knowledge of the civilization and language of the Ancient Egyptians was lost for many centuries, the impressive monuments of this great people remained a source of amazement and curiosity to all Europeans who traveled to Egypt.

Greek and Roman writers recorded their journeys and, throughout medieval times, pilgrims passed through Egypt on their way to the Holy Land. By the eighteenth century, many travelers had published accounts of their journeys. These often included detailed illustrations of the amazing things they saw.

These images of Ancient Egypt appeared alien to Europeans, who were more familiar with their classical heritage. The languages of this heritage, Greek and Latin, had been maintained, and its art and architecture had enjoyed fashionable revivals. The mysterious hieroglyphs, weird, animal-headed gods and exotic costumes of Ancient Egypt appeared to Europeans of the past, as they do to us nowadays, very strange indeed.

STUDYING ANCIENT EGYPT

The first major study of Ancient Egyptian civilization was undertaken by a group of French scholars who accompanied Napoleon's Egyptian campaign in 1798. They took with them artists to record what they saw and they eventually published a whole series of beautifully illustrated volumes called *Description de L'Egypte*.

At this time the French Army discovered a stone at a place called Rosetta, which had the same text inscribed on it in Greek, hieroglyphics and another Egyptian text called Demotic. After 20 years of dedicated study, this inscription was to provide the Frenchman, Jean-François Champollion (1790-1832), with the key to deciphering the hieroglyphs. The decipherment of the script, which took place between 1822 and 1824, and the publication of the multivolume work, *Description de L'Egypte* (1809-30), mark the beginning of Egyptology as a separate subject.

INSPIRING THE WORLD

After his success with understanding the hieroglyphs, Champollion mounted a joint expedition with an Italian called Rossellini to record the Egyptian monuments in detail. As a result they each produced beautifully illustrated publications which, together with the *Description de L'Egypte*, did much to popularize Ancient Egypt throughout Europe.

They also inspired more travelers and merchants to visit Egypt. These people were attracted not only by eager curiosity but by the

Opposite: A map showing the historical sites of Ancient Egypt. These sites have yielded incredible treasures of a golden age, and have provided future generations with an insight into how the Ancient Egyptians lived.

Left: Jean-François Champollion (1790-1832) – the "Father of Egyptology" and the decipherer of hieroglyphs.

Above: Giovanni Belzoni (1778-1823), an Italian excavator, explorer, and adventurer who was the most colorful character in nineteenth-century Egyptology.

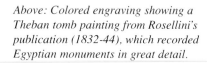

Above: Colored engraving showing a Theban tomb painting from Rosellini's publication (1832-44), which recorded Egyptian monuments in great detail.

opportunity to return with antiquities which were becoming valuable. We should not forget that at this time travel to Egypt was lengthy and hazardous, and the inhabitants were not particularly friendly to Europeans, while the climate and prevalence of serious diseases added to the difficulty.

THE EXPLORERS

The most colorful personality to be involved with Egyptology at this time was an Italian called Giovanni Belzoni (1778-1823). He had

at one time been a strongman performer in the London theater and had traveled to Egypt to work as an engineer. These skills led him to become involved in the removal of a colossal bust of Ramses II, which he successfully transported to the British Museum in London in 1818.

This project was commissioned by Henry Salt, the British consul in Egypt. Salt himself became a keen collector of Egyptian antiquities and his collection, with the help of Belzoni, was to form the nucleus of that of the British Museum. They were both involved in lengthy and frustrating final negotiations with the trustees of the museum, who disputed the value of some of the sculptures. The main problem was that many people tended to

Above: Portrait of Henry Salt (1780-1827), the British consul in Egypt whose important collection of antiquities formed the basis of the British Museum's Egyptian collection. (British Museum.)

Above: A drawing by Giovanni Belzoni showing the transportation of a colossal bust of Ramses II which became part of the British Museum collection. Belzoni's successful direction of the transportation of such a heavy statue to England was a remarkable achievement.

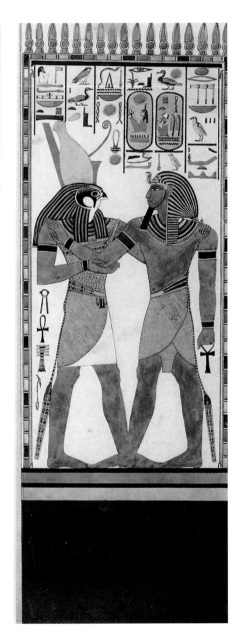

Right: A colored drawing of painted reliefs from the tomb of Seti I by Henry Salt (1780-1827), the British consul in Egypt. He was a keen collector, responsible for obtaining some of the British Museum's major sculptures, and was also a skilled amateur artist. (British Museum.)

Left: A view of the Ramesseum, Thebes, in the nineteenth century by Francis Frith (1822-98), one of the most notable British pioneer photographers who traveled to Egypt.

Below: Collection of pots from the publication Description de l'Egypte *(1809-30) which recorded Egyptian antiquities in unprecedented detail.*

regard Egyptian statues as greatly inferior to classical, as being merely curiosities rather than works of art.

Belzoni went on to complete some successful excavations in Egypt, discovering an entrance to the Second Pyramid and the tomb of Seti I, in the Valley of the Kings. He also traveled far south to the great temple of Abu Simbel in Nubia, which he was the first to enter since ancient times. He published a popular account of these exploits in four different languages, and went on to stage a spectacular exhibition at the Egyptian Hall in Piccadilly, in 1821.

Sir John Gardner Wilkinson is generally regarded as the founder of British Egyptology. He spent many years in Egypt copying paintings and inscriptions, and mastering the ancient language. He was the first to attempt placing the royal dynasties and kings into proper date order, and he gave many important antiquities to the British Museum. He popularized Egyptology with his best-known book *The Manners and Customs of the Ancient Egyptians* (1837), which became the standard work on religion, daily life, and culture for many years. Another key figure in Egyptology at this time was Robert Hay, who, like Wilkinson, was not funded by any organization. He financed a number of important expeditions resulting in detailed studies.

This essential, serious, survey work eventually gained official interest and, during the 1840s, the King of Prussia financed a large-scale expedition to the Nile. This was led by the capable Karl Lepsius, who secured some major antiquities for the future Berlin Museum and produced a lavish publication of 24 volumes, entitled *Denkmaeler*. This is the largest work on Egyptology ever published, and is still a valuable and highly regarded reference work for scholars today.

PROTECTING THE TREASURES

Egyptologists had been largely concerned with dating and language, and excavating had been undertaken in an unscientific way. Many inscriptions and papyri were destroyed in an eager search for more attractive antiquities, while unscrupulous dealers had little regard as to how they gained access to tombs.

A Frenchman called Auguste Mariette, who was collecting antiquities for the Louvre Museum, realized the need to prevent indiscriminate looting of sites and set up an official antiquities service for the Egyptians. Mariette ensured that excavation permits were only issued to qualified scholars, and went on to found the Cairo Museum. A new standard of orderly, scientific archaeology was set by W. M. F. Petrie, who excavated all over Egypt, publishing a detailed record and analysis of the finds almost every year between 1881 and 1925.

THE VALLEY OF THE KINGS

In the 1870s a pit was discovered at Thebes containing the mummies of most of the New Kingdom pharaohs. These had been removed from their original tombs in antiquity by the priests and reburied to prevent their violation by tomb robbers. Archeologists turned their attention to exploring the Valley of the Kings

Right: Frontispiece from the publication Description de l'Egypte *(1809-30), showing French soldiers among the ancient ruins.*

Above: W. M . F. Petrie (1853-1942), the most active archeologist working in Egypt, pioneered new scientific methods and produced some 1000 publications.

at Thebes to locate the original tombs. Howard Carter, a former assistant of Petrie, began excavating there in 1912 under the sponsorship of Lord Carnarvon. Eventually, in 1922, he discovered the tomb of Tutankhamun, the first pharaoh's tomb to be found virtually intact. The incredible wealth of gold and the superb artistic craftsmanship displayed in all this treasure attracted massive media coverage, which really captured people's imagination about Ancient Egypt.

SETTLEMENT SITES

Beside tombs, archeologists excavated settlement sites in order to find out more about the Egyptians' daily life. The most important discoveries in this field have been at the ancient city of El-Amarna and the workmen's village of Deir el-Medina. At El-Amarna, a German team led by Ludwig Borchardt discovered the famous bust of Nefertiti while excavating a sculptor's workshop. Large-scale archeological surveys have been of great importance to Egyptology, initiated by the work of Norman de Garis Davies (1865-1941). He became the greatest copyist of Egyptian tombs and published more than 25 volumes on tombs alone, while his wife Nina made beautiful colored reproductions of the wall paintings.

The most important work of this type to follow Davies was done by the University of Chicago, which has a base at Luxor called The Chicago House. This organization, founded by James Breasted, has published an exhaustive record of the important temples at Medinet Habu and Abydos.

Many specialized societies have also been founded which sponsor excavations in Egypt and publish regular journals. One of the most famous is the Egypt Exploration Society, which

Above: Auguste Mariette (1821-81) formed the Egyptian Antiquities service and founded the Cairo Museum. He directed many important excavations and published many books on Egyptology.

has a distinguished history of fieldwork, and offers its members a means of keeping in touch with the very latest developments in Egyptological research.

TREASURES UNDER THREAT

Although the treasures of Tutankhamun were handed over to the Cairo Museum, the Egyptian government has been somewhat restrictive in granting permits to excavate since this discovery. They are naturally anxious not to lose any more of their cultural heritage, and scholars and museums have found sponsorship difficult since they are not allowed to keep what they excavate.

From the 1950s onward, Egyptian universities and the Egyptian antiquities organizations have themselves excavated many sites and published an increasing amount of research material. However, in the 1960s, the Egyptians appealed to the world to help them save their important Nubian monuments from the flooding due to the construction of the Aswan High Dam. An international consortium of contractors and archeologists was set up to move the huge temple of Abu Simbel and some other monuments to higher ground.

The rescue project has inspired detailed surveys of sites under threat from the floodwaters and greater interest in Nubia. Scholars now treat Nubian studies as a separate branch of Egyptology, with current research concentrating on the earliest settlements and the Kingdom of Meroe, which survived into the fourth century A.D.

THE LANGUAGE

Work in Egypt itself is only a small part of Egyptology, and much has been achieved by studying collections of antiquities distributed throughout world museums. Understanding the language has always been of major importance to Egyptologists, and they can learn a great deal from reading the large quantity of texts that have survived written on stone monuments, papyrus, and pottery and limestone ostraca fragments.

The most useful textbook for students of the language is the famous *Egyptian Grammar* by Sir Alan Gardiner. First published in 1927, it has enabled generations of Egyptologists to study the hieroglyphic script. Great advances have been made in reading the difficult Demotic script, and many texts await translation and publication. These may give us some fresh information about the Ancient Egyptians.

MODERN EGYPTOLOGY

Nowadays, Ancient Egypt can be studied at various levels at universities, colleges, schools, and adult-education institutes. It can be taken as a separate degree subject or combined with ancient history, archeology, art history, classics or language studies. Many museums, societies and adult-education institutes also offer lecture programs with slides, films, and videos. Egypt itself is becoming increasingly popular and affordable to tourists, and certain companies provide special study holidays which include cruises down the Nile with guest Egyptologists and expert guides to accompany the tours.

Modern Egyptologists have far greater study

Top: Howard Carter and his team of archeologists in the Valley of the Kings just before their famous discovery in 1922.

Below: The Temple of Abu Simbel, *by Scottish artist and traveler David Roberts (1796-1864).*

resources than their predecessors. They have dictionaries, lists of kings, and detailed site surveys to help them with their research. Study of museum collections has also greatly improved through better documentation of the artifacts on computers and detailed photographic archives. Fresh knowledge can often be gained by using the latest scientific techniques to help with dating and analysis of the material. There is greater contact between Egyptologists internationally through specialist conferences and the current popularity of loan exhibitions of Egyptian antiquities.

Ancient Egypt covered a long period of history and a vast geographical area. So much has already been achieved by Egyptologists – yet there are some periods of history and many pharaohs that we know little or nothing about. Research on existing collections is continuing – there must be countless antiquities still to be excavated and studied.

Above: Although there are only a few obelisks still standing in Egypt, there are more than 50 in the public squares of capitals in Europe and America. (David Roberts lithograph, c. 1846.)

Left: The Tomb of Queen Nefertari, – watercolor copy by Nina Davies (1881-1965). Records like these are invaluable ,since many tomb paintings have deteriorated greatly since their discovery.

Above: Travel brochure from the 1920s. Since the major ancient sites are easily accessible from the river, the Nile cruise has become the most leisurely way to tour Egypt.

ANCIENT EGYPTIAN LIFE

*A fine-quality stool made of ebony and ivory with a
leather-covered seat.
(British Museum.)*

Much can be learned about the life of the Ancient Egyptians from the everyday items and wall-paintings to be found in their tombs. The Egyptians believed that these representations of work and pleasure would assist them in the afterlife. Many tombs and temples have survived from ancient times because they were made of stone. Few houses remain since they were built from perishable materials, like mud-brick, which collapsed when it was old, and is now used as a fertilizer. Many towns and villages continued to be inhabited throughout history until modern times, and houses were frequently rebuilt and the material recycled. Many modern Egyptian villages probably resemble the ancient ones quite closely in their construction and way of life. Occasionally, settlements were completely abandoned, and excavating them can tell us a great deal about the daily lives of the ordinary people.

Above: The workmen's village at Deir-el-Medina. This is one of the most important Ancient Egyptian sites, revealing how ordinary workers lived.

Egyptian towns and cities served two main purposes: they were centers of government and centers of trade. Egypt was divided, for government and taxation, into 42 districts called "nomes." There was a leading town in each nome. In addition, certain major cities, such as Memphis and Thebes, acted as national capitals throughout Egyptian history. The pharoahs built splendid palaces at both Memphis and Thebes.

HOMES TO THE GODS

Many cities were also the home of a god, or, according to Egyptian religious belief, were regularly visited by one. The Egyptians believed in many local gods, "the spirits of the place," who often took the form of typical local animals. The hawk-headed god, Horus, for example, was particularly sacred to the inhabitants of Heliopolis.

Other cities housed the shrines of major, national gods. At Thebes, for example, there was a magnificent group of temples dedicated to the god Amun. In the desert that lies beyond the opposite river bank, there were many royal tombs. Pharaoh Akhenaten built a whole new capital, "the city of the sun-disk," at a site now known as El-Amarna, not far from Thebes. But his religious reforms were rejected after his death, and the beautiful new city was abandoned and left to ruin.

Memphis, in particular, was a great center of trade. It lay along the bank of the River Nile, which led northward toward the Mediterranean Sea. Merchants from many lands – Syria, Palestine, Libya, Phoenecia, Cyprus, and Sicily – came to its busy harbor and traded and settled there, creating an international business community.

Egyptian traders purchased copper, incense and semiprecious stones, such as turquoise and lapis lazuli, as well as timber for building temples and ships, and fine-quality cedar wood. In return, they exported corn, lentils, papyrus and linen. Because there was no common currency, or money, international merchants would have exchanged or bartered with different goods or produce.

The two most notable Ancient Egyptian sites to be excavated are King Akhenaten's city at El-Amarna, and the village of the workmen who built the tombs in the Valley of the Kings at Deir-el-Medina. This village grew over four centuries. Rectangular walls originally enclosed the streets and houses, which were laid out in a regular pattern. The individual houses were roughly the same size except for the larger houses of the foremen.

EGYPTIAN HOUSES

A typical house had three main rooms, with a yard which acted as a kitchen, and two cellars intended for storage. There were often niches set into the walls for religious stone inscriptions, images of household gods or busts of family ancestors. Many houses came to be modified to suit individual needs or activities and some included workrooms and shops. At El-Amarna, the finer houses had two floors and basement storerooms. They sometimes also had a reception hall, kitchen, and servants' quarters, while some even had bathrooms and toilet facilities. A number of walled houses

Right: Pottery tomb model of a house with a window and a roof which acts as a wind-vent to catch the breeze. In the forecourt are various provisions. c. 1900 B.C. (British Museum.)

HOMES THEN AND NOW

The Egyptians invented many important construction methods, many of which are still used today.
Top: Mud-brick arches in storerooms built at Thebes around 3100 years ago.
Below: A modern building near Luxor, which uses very similar techniques.

had an enclosed garden with a fish pond and several shady trees.

Furniture consisted of beds, small tables, stools, and wooden storage chests for utensils and jewelry. Hangings, mats, and textiles decorated the inner rooms. Like many African peoples, the Egyptians used headrests instead of pillows for sleeping on. Many of these headrests, made from either wood, ivory, or stone, have survived. They consist of a curved neckpiece set on top of a pillar which sits on an oblong base.

The house also contained lamps, which were simple bowls of pottery or stone containing oil and a wick. They also used pottery torches which could be set into brackets on the wall. Kitchens and cellars had clay ovens and large storage jars for wine, oil, and grain.

LIFE FOR THE WORKERS

The workmen who lived at Deir-el-Medina were stonemasons, plasterers, sculptors, draughtsmen, painters, and carpenters. The valley contains the remains of their houses, tombs, chapels, rest-houses and domestic trash. Many written documents have been discovered there which deal with the progress of the work, and there is even the earliest record of a strike, caused by a delay in paying the workers' wages.

The men would have worked for eight days out of ten, living in huts above the Valley of the Kings and returning to the village for their two days of rest. Attendance registers have survived and we know that absenteeism was common. Days were lost through brewing beer, drinking, and building houses, and there were

A pottery lamp used for cooking, for cosmetics, and for lighting. This lamp burned olive oil.

also many religious holidays. Their wages were paid in wheat, fish, vegetables, cosmetic oils, wood for fuel, pottery, and clothing. The workers used each other's skills to construct highly decorated tombs for themselves, and there were also many opportunities to undertake private commissions from wealthy Thebans.

Many legal documents have survived from Deir-el-Medina concerning crimes and judgements, inheritances, and business transactions. The Ancient Egyptians had a legal system of courts and magistrates, and they had a wide range of punishments, which included forced labor camps. They had a type of police force, distinct from the army, which often used trained dogs. There existed a system of giving evidence under oath, and documents often contain signatures of witnesses. Documents were legalized by affixing a seal, and were deposited at a record office or temple.

The Ancient Egyptians had schools, but these would have been for training future scribes and officials intended for the priesthood or the civil administration, who were exclusively male. The royal family had special tutors, and ordinary people were educated at home. The father traditionally handed down advice and professional secrets to his son relating to his trade or craft. Craftsmen, like officials, had an apprenticeship system.

WORKING THE LAND

The majority of the population was engaged in working on the land, and people's labor was conscripted for irrigation systems or royal building projects. This conscription was for everyone, although privileged officials could avoid it by paying someone else to work on their behalf. Foreign prisoners-of-war and

Below left: Painted wooden model of a man plowing. (British Museum.)

Below right: Wealthy Egyptians had many servants, both men and women. This graceful statue shows a woman servant carrying a heavy box., c. 2020 B.C.

Above: Painted wooden model of bread-makers, c. 2000 B.C. (British Museum.)

Opposite:Blue-glazed drinking-cup in the form of a lotus. (British Museum.)

criminals were also used in gangs for heavier work like stone-quarrying.

Conscripted workers received no payment for their services, only subsistence. Even the poorest peasant laborers and domestic servants were not slaves in the usual sense of the word. All Egyptians had legal rights and could own or dispose of their possessions. There was no system of citizenship or slavery, as clearly defined in Greece and Rome. Egyptian society never produced a true

middle class, and the social structure was a hierarchy of officials. In this hierarchy, everyone ultimately served the pharaoh, who was the embodiment of the state.

PRODUCE AND TRADE

Working the land was vital. In addition to cereals, flax was grown in great quantities, to be spun into thread, and finally woven into linen. Large herds of cattle were reared and cows dragged the plow and provided milk.

Other livestock kept included sheep, pigs, and donkeys. Surplus agricultural produce and linen were exported by the royal government, which controlled trade.

In country markets, barter or exchange was the means of trade. The Ancient Egyptians managed without coinage during their long history. They had a system of valuing provisions and manufactured articles in various units equivalent to fixed amounts of gold, silver or copper. Payments could be made either in given weights or rings of the metal itself – unlike coins, these pieces had no official markings as a guarantee of value – or commodities such as produce or livestock.

FAMILY LIFE

The family was at the heart of Egyptian society. For many Egyptians, especially women, family life was important because their house was also their place of work. Indoors, women and their older daughters cooked, cleaned and cared for young children. They used the courtyards of their homes for grinding corn, drying fish, plucking waterfowl, baking bread, and brewing beer.

During busy seasons, women would also help their husbands and brothers, who were out working in the fields. This involved weeding crops, feeding animals, and gathering in the harvest. They might also spin thread and weave rough fabric for the family's clothes. Egyptian women made most of the clothes for their families to wear.

SHORT LIVES

Life expectancy was severely limited for the Egyptians. Today, most of us can expect to live until we are about 70 years old. This was not the case for ancient Egyptians. Then, life expectancy was short: on average, people lived for 20 years. This suggests that many people died very young, some lived to perhaps 30 or 40, and a few lived longer. There are no precise figures, but it is likely that many, if not most, babies died before they reached their fifth birthday. Only the strongest survived.

These figures had an effect on family life. People got married much younger; for example, Tutankhamun married when he was only ten. The Egyptians must also have got used to the frequent death of babies and toddlers. The threat of disease, brought into Egyptian homes by rats, mice, and insects, was constant. From the evidence of mummies, Egyptians seemed to have suffered from several unpleasant conditions – from diarrhea and worms to sores and blindness – all caught from animals.

LOVE AND MARRIAGE

Early marriage and parenthood were encouraged. Many marriages would have been arranged, but the romantic nature of surviving love poetry suggests that there was some freedom of choice. Marriage tended to be within the same social group, and family unions between uncle and niece or cousins were common. The words "brother" and "sister" were often used merely as terms of endearment in their writings, and have led to a misconception that the Egyptians committed incest. There was no religious or civil marriage ceremony, although there were family parties and festivities to celebrate the occasion.

Marriage was a private legal agreement, and a contract established the right of both parties to maintenance and possessions. There was consequently an equality between men and women in their opportunity to own, manage, and receive property. If there was a divorce, the rights of the wife were protected equally with those of her husband. In some periods of Egyptian history, even a woman who committed adultery still had certain rights to maintenance from her former husband.

In spite of the formal legal contract of marriage with the facility for divorce, marriages were not usually short-lived or lacking in affection. Many statues and wall-paintings show married couples displaying gestures of affection for each other, and their surviving literature often suggests sincere emotional ties.

FOOD

The average Egyptian peasant probably lived on a few rolls of bread, a pot of beer, and some onions. The staple food was always bread and by the time of the New Kingdom there were as many as 40 different varieties. The

Egyptians had 15 different words for bread. The shapes of the loaves varied: some were oval and some were round, while others were conical. Bread was made from an early form of wheat, emmer wheat, ground between millstones or in a hand-held quern. Egyptian bread was made without yeast, so it was flat and quickly became stale. It may have looked like the pitta bread we can buy today. Different flours and honey, milk and eggs, were sometimes added.

Beside the cereals from which bread was made, the fertile soil around the Nile provided many varieties of fresh fruit and vegetables, including melons, leeks, onions, radishes, garlic, and cucumbers. Figs, dates, pomegranates, and grapes were among the quantities of fruit available. Farms provided milk and dairy products, and they hatched eggs artificially. Honey, produced from bee-keeping, played a large part in the Egyptians' diet as a sugar substitute.

Other staple foods included beans, onions, and dried meat. Meat included beef, goat, mutton, pork, goose, and pigeon. Wild birds like geese and ducks were caught and eaten. However, meat would not keep in the hot climate and had to be consumed rapidly, so for most people it would only be eaten on religious feast days. Fish was eaten more frequently, particularly among the people living around the marshes.

Metal was precious in Ancient Egypt. Bowls and pots for cooking were therefore made of clay. They ate from plates made of pottery, sometimes decorated with trailing clay patterns. Jars were used to store oil, wine, beer, or water. They were made from local clay by skilled Egyptian potters.

DRINKING

To drink, there was river water, beer, or wine for the rich. Beer was the most popular drink. It was probably safer than plain water, since the alcohol it contained acted as a mild disinfectant. It was prepared from barley which

Below: This knife, used to prepare food, was made of flint. Its edge is surprisingly sharp.

Above: Painted wooden model of a woman carrying a tray of cakes.

Right: Metal was precious in Ancient Egypt. Bowls and pots for cooking were therefore made of clay.

Far right: This basket sieve was used to strain beverages like beer, which could not be drunk before straining as it was so gritty.

Right: Men picking grapes to make wine, from a Theban tomb painting.

MAKING BEER FROM BREAD

Above: This model shows beer-making. The brewer is bending over a large pottery vat, stirring crumbs of part-baked bread into river water.

was ground, kneaded, and mixed with plenty of water to make a dough, and then lightly baked like bread. The brewer used a large pottery vat, into which he stirred crumbs of part-baked bread into river water.

Often, this process was done by men standing inside the vat, trampling the bread and water with their feet. After mixing, the liquid was left to stand in the sun, until it fermented. Then it was strained, and stored in pottery jars in the sunshine.

It must have looked like a very muddy soup. Perhaps understandably, some people liked to strain it before drinking. Many pottery beer-strainers have been found. Although women performed most household tasks, brewing seems, from the evidence of models and carvings, to have been a male speciality. The Egyptians also made wine, and various regions were noted for their quality. It was stored in pottery jars and had a label noting its origin, maker, and date. There were many accounts of drunkenness, especially after excessive banquets and parties.

FEASTS AND FESTIVALS

Food was important in religious festivals and seasonal celebrations. Paintings in tombs show pharoahs and wealthy families feasting on roast duck, beef, honey-cakes, fruits and wine. Not everyone could afford this level of luxury. At a feast, diners were waited on by servants, and entertained by musicians, acrobats, and dancing girls. To complete the festive mood, the women carried sweet-smelling lotus blossoms, or wore cones of perfumed grease.

CLOTHES

We know a lot about the clothing the Ancient Egyptians wore, since it is depicted in countless sculptures and paintings. Many examples of actual clothing have also been discovered amongst other tomb artifacts. A large number of textiles were found in Tutankhamun's tomb, including over a hundred loin cloths and about 30 gloves or chariot-driving gauntlets. The world's earliest surviving dress made of stitched linen, was discovered at Tarkhan in Egypt, and dates from 2800 B.C. White linen was the standard material for clothing as it was cool and light to wear. Garments were often carefully pleated and they were

Below: A group of female musicians playing a harp, lute, flute, and lyre.

Right: A woman wearing a dress of the style worn by officials and dignitaries at the end of the Middle Kingdom. (British Museum.)

Far right: Lady'svanity box containing a selection of cosmetics vessels, toilet objects and pair of sandals. (British Museum.)

draped around the body rather than tailored, with minimum stitching. Simple ankle-length sheath dresses were worn. In the New Kingdom, they were often more pleated, and fringes became popular. Women also sometimes wore an elegant, heavily pleated, fringed robe over this dress.

Men usually wore a short kilt, made from a rectangular piece of linen folded round the body and tied or fastened at the waist. This was sometimes starched at the front to form an apron, or pleated. Occasionally they would wear a cloak in cooler weather. Working men wore only a loincloth while children are often depicted naked. The wealthy

WIG

Above: This statue shows a woman wearing a short wig. Ancient Egyptians often wore wigs.

Right: Wooden box inlaid with colored ivory and a selection of typical Egyptian jewelry and amulets. (British Museum.)

had a type of laundry service with meticulous methods of washing and pleating, and numerous laundry lists and marks on clothing have survived. Sandals made from woven reed, grass, or leather, sometimes upturned like Turkish slippers, were also worn.

Elaborate and colorful jewelry contrasted well with the usually plain garments. Jewelry was worn both for personal adornment and as a protection against evil. The most characteristic form of jewelry was the collar, which was composed of numerous strings of beads using attractive stones like carnelian, jasper, and lapis lazuli. Armlets, bracelets, and anklets were worn, while finger rings often included seals. In the New Kingdom, both men and women had pierced ears, and a wide variety of earrings and ear studs survive. There are many hairstyles depicted in sculpture and

wall-paintings, with fashions varying according to the period. Men usually wore a rounded hairstyle that followed the line of their heads. They were generally clean-shaven, and razors were used from the earliest times in Egypt. The priests shaved their heads, as did the wealthier men and women, who wore wigs. These were mainly of human hair with some vegetable-fiber padding. Some wigs have survived that are composed of an intricate assortment of curls and plaits, sometimes with attached bead ornaments.

COSMETICS

The Egyptians were very fond of cosmetics and men, women, and children used facial make-up called kohl to create a dark line round the eyes. Beside being decorative, kohl protected the eyes against infection and stopped

the glare of the sun. Red ocher was used to color the cheeks, and probably also as lipstick, while henna was used as a hair colorant. Countless bronze mirrors have survived – which would originally have been highly polished – and also a large variety of cosmetic vessels, spoons, and applicators.

EGYPTIAN TOILETRIES

Medical papyri mention recipes for creams and oils to keep the skin soft and supple after exposure to the hot Egyptian sun. Perfumes, some of which took months to prepare, were popular and were also worn by men during certain festivals. A popular form of incense cone was worn by women on top of the head at banquets to perfume the wig and garments.

Below: An ivory case which contained kohl, and a make-up palette for mixing eye-shadow color.
Right: Pharaohs and their wives enjoyed wearing splendid clothes, jewels, wigs, and make-up, to reflect their power.

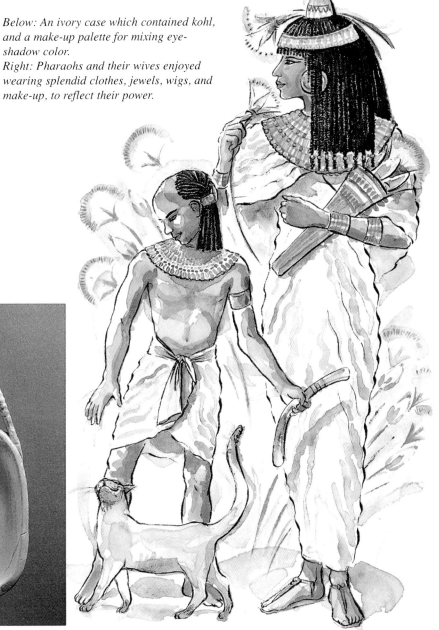

ART AND CRAFTS

Technical skill was greatly admired, but there was no distinction between artists and craftsmen, and therefore art is generally anonymous. Craftsmen were employed by the king or the temple officials, and their achievement and skill using simple tools is remarkable. Like Egyptian farmers, they achieved great success using very simple tools. The materials they worked with were not easy to manipulate. Even so, they managed to produce a high level of finish on carvings, statues, jewelry, and other decorative objects.

Their most impressive achievements were in sculpture, both in the round, and in carved relief. They also mastered the technique of making fine stone vessels from an early date. The precision of their carpentry was also very fine, and wood was joined by dovetailing, miters, mortise-and-tenon joints and dowels. Inlay and veneer were common forms of decoration, and the Egyptians were the first to use plywood. Their tools, which would have been copper, included axs, saws, chisels, and drills. The wood, much of which was imported, was mainly cedar, sycamore, acacia, ebony and palmwood.

HANDLING MATERIALS

Metal-workers and jewelers showed a high degree of skill in using techniques like chasing, engraving, embossing, inlaying, filigree work, and enameling. They could beat gold into leaf as fine as 0.005 mm, and gemstones and beads of small sizes were bored with precision using a bow drill. Copper was smelted using a type of bellows, and bronze was cast by the lost-wax process. These materials were essential for making tools, weapons, ritual utensils, and religious statuettes.

Another characteristic Egyptian craft technique was the manufacture of glass and glazed ware. Faience ware, usually of blue-green or turquoise glaze, was produced in vast quantities, often from molds. The Egyptians could also produce linen of outstanding quality, and a shawl discovered in Tutankhamun's tomb is made of the finest linen known. Textile experts have estimated that it must have taken about 3000 hours to make, or nine months of 11-hour days. Allied to weaving was the manufacture of mats, baskets, and rope using reed, flax, papyrus, palm fiber, and grass. Countless baskets and pottery have survived which were the standard household containers.

TOWARD EXPERIMENTATION

In most periods of Egyptian history, artists and craftsmen were content to copy, or slightly improve upon, earlier styles. They followed well-established traditions, which showed respect for pharaohs and the gods. Change for its own sake was not particularly valued; many people preferred something familiar to something new. But slowly, innovations did take place. Statues of famous people were carved in new poses, and painters began to depict animals, gods, and people in experimental styles.

In Memphis and Thebes, there were many busy craftsmen, all specialists in a particular trade. Paintings from Theban tombs portray a wide variety of crafts. There were leather-workers, sandal-makers, stone-carvers, metal-workers, chariot-makers, sculptors, carpenters, jewelers, scribes, and boat-builders in the sixth-dynasty (around 2200 B.C) tomb alone.

Many of these craftsmen would have worked mainly for pharaohs or for wealthy noble or merchant families. But, when they

Left: A detail from a wall-painting in a Theban tomb, showing jewelers and carpenters hard at work.

had surplus goods to spare, villagers traveled into the towns to exchange their agricultural produce for these finely made objects. Many towns had regular markets and occasional festivals, usually connected with the Nile flood season, good harvests, or a favorite local god.

METALWORKING

Some of the finest Egyptian statues were made of bronze, for example, a model of the sacred bull, Apis, who was worshiped in the city of Memphis. Several steps were involved in making a statue from bronze, or from any other metal. First, a mold was made, usually of clay. This was a hollowed-out block, divided into two halves. Each half showed all the details that would appear on the surface of the finished statue. When the mold was ready, the two halves were joined together using more clay. Then the ready-mixed metal – bronze is a mixture of copper and tin – was melted over a hot fire. Very carefully, it was poured into

the mold; the smallest splashes could cause a nasty burn. It was then left to cool. This took several days. Finally, the mold was split open, and the finished cast was trimmed and polished. A new work of art was complete. Skillful workmen could use the same mold over again, to make more copies of the same statue. But, for large pieces, this was not often done. The amount of metal needed to make a solid statue was very expensive. And not many pharaohs wanted their image to be mass-produced.

LEISURE TIME

The Egyptians depicted many of their favorite pastimes in their tombs because they wanted to enjoy them forever in the afterlife. Hunting was popular among the nobility and the wealthy. Athletic games and sports were often group activities and these included wrestling, boxing, stave-fighting, ball games, gymnastics and acrobatics. Many paintings

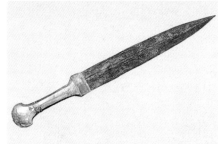

Left: These delicate Egyptian glass vases were made around 350 B.C.

Top: Craftsmen at work. This painting from the tomb of the noble Rekhmire shows carpenters, potters, and goldsmiths working at their trades.

Above: A gold-handled dagger, fashioned by skilled Egyptian craftsmen. (British Museum.)

have survived of banqueting scenes where acrobats and dancers performed. The pirouette and some other ballet movements were known to the Ancient Egyptians, and dancing with rhythmic accompaniment from clapping, cymbals, sistra, bells, and chanting was also popular at religious festivals.

MUSIC AND GAMES

Music was an essential accompaniment to dance, but it was also practised in its own right. The harp and the flute were often played, together with various wind instruments with and without reeds. These were made from wood or metal. Probably the earliest-known account of a full orchestra performing a concert dates from *c.* 250 B.C. This was at a large festival for Pharaoh Ptolemy II, where 600 musicians played simultaneously.

The Egyptians also played board games. The most popular game was called "Senet," and many highly decorative boards with counters have survived, usually made of wood and ivory. Some boards have an alternative game on the other side, which was called "Twenty Squares." There were also games called "Serpent," and "Dog," and the "Jackal." Children amused themselves with a variety of toys, which included balls, tops, dolls, and figures of animals with movable parts.

Bottom left: Tomb paintings show dancing girls entertaining pharoahs and their courtiers at feasts.

Bottom right: A man and his wife playing the board game senet – from a papyrus, c. 1,250 BC. (British Museum.)

THE
RIVER NILE

Sunset over the River Nile – the life-blood
of Ancient Egypt.

Without the Nile, Egypt would not exist. There would be no water, and no fertile land to grow food. Egyptian rainfall is low; only about 100-150 m.m. in an average year. The climate is hot. Even in winter, the temperatures seldom fall below 13 degrees centigrade. The surrounding desert lands show the natural results of weather conditions like these.

One of the world's greatest rivers, the Nile flows for a vast distance in a valley bordered by rocky cliffs and hills. Flowing for over 4000 miles (6500 km), the Nile is the longest river in the world. It is formed from two great streams, the Blue Nile, which rises in Ethiopia, and the White Nile, which rises in Uganda. They join at Khartoum to become the main river which runs north through the desert to the Mediterranean Sea. Along its course, the river is interrupted at six points by rapids or cataracts, and the first of these, near Aswan, marks the Nile's entry into Egypt proper. For the last hundred-odd miles the river fans out in tributaries over the marshy flats of the Delta. This northern region of Egypt, which includes the Delta, is known as Lower Egypt. The part to the south of it, called Upper Egypt, is quite different geographically. Here the land is drier, and the river is bordered on both sides by cliffs.

THE FLOODING OF THE NILE

Once a year, between July and October, the main stream of the Nile, charged with torrential Ethiopian rainfall, traditionally distributed its water over Egypt. When the water receded, it left behind a thick, fertile layer of mud and silt covering the valley floor. Over many centuries, this had built up into a layer of damp, warm, rich soil. The Ancient Egyptians called this the "black land" to distinguish it from the "red land" of the desert. This is where they lived and grew their crops.

When the river flooded, its banks became submerged under the water. Egyptian farmers planted grains, lentils, beans, and vegetables in the wet Nile mud as soon as the flood waters went down. Crops grew quickly, and gave good yields. The fresh silt every year acted as a natural fertilizer. Egyptian farmers probably made and mended many of their own agricultural tools. These were often very simple, and were constructed of wood. But they did the job well, if the men – or sometimes women – using them knew what they were doing and worked hard. There was no time to waste.

The farmers used oxen to pull their wooden plows. If they could not afford to keep animals, then they dug the rich black mud by hand, using digging sticks and hoes. Plowing and reaping took place at the same time. The plowman drove cattle and the sower walked behind him scattering seed. At the time for harvest, crops were cut down using sickles. However, if, as occasionally happened, the Nile floods failed, there was famine in the land.

It was also important to try and exterminate the pests that threatened their crops. Mice and locusts were particularly destructive. The Egyptians kept – and sometimes worshiped – cats; a few, belonging to noble sportsmen, were even trained to retrieve birds that were killed with sticks. Cats killed the mice, but nothing could defend the fields from a swarm of hungry locusts. If they arrived before harvest time, then, as one Egyptian poet wrote,

Left: This tomb painting shows Sennedjem plowing with a pair of oxen. He is driving them forward with a double whip. His wife walks beside him.

Above: This ox was carved on the wall of the temple of Ramses II at Abydos. It came from the temple's own farms, and had been specially bred and fattened up. Now, in peak condition, it is shown taking part in a festival procession, on its way to be slaughtered as an offering to the gods.

"the rich look worried, and every man is seen to be carrying his weapons." Making sure of a good harvest was a matter of life and death.

A SOURCE OF FOOD

The Nile itself provided food. Fish were trapped in wide nets thrown by fishermen, or caught with hooks and lines by anglers sitting on floating papyrus rafts. Plants grew along the river bank and were cut down for use. For example, rushes were used to weave matting and baskets. Lotus blossoms were gathered to decorate rich people's baskets. Ferries and cargo boats steered a careful course through the winding river channels. Cows, donkeys, rats, dogs, and small children paddled in the waters at the river's edge. Women gathered to wash dirty clothes, chatting and laughing together. Drinking water was drawn straight from sewage-polluted shallows. The "river of life" was also a breeding ground for disease.

As well as laboring in the fields, Egyptian villagers gathered clover and other wild plants to feed their cattle, and cut rushes to make baskets and mats. They reared ducks and geese.

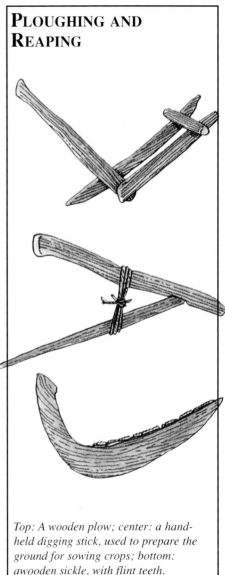

PLOUGHING AND REAPING

Top: A wooden plow; center: a hand-held digging stick, used to prepare the ground for sowing crops; bottom: a wooden sickle, with flint teeth.

They spun wool to make thread, and grew flax in muddy pools. Both were used to weave cloth. Where there was enough land, they planted orchards and vineyards, and harvested apples, grapes, and figs. They used the Nile mud to make bricks to build and repair their homes.

The land around the Nile Delta was particularly fertile, and the marshland was teeming with wild life. Large areas of the marsh came to be carefully preserved for hunting, cattle-raising, wild fruits, and fishing. Fishing was a prosperous occupation, and those who lived on the edge of the marshes were organized into teams for fishing. The most effective method was to drag a great trawl-net between two boats and bring it to the bank. However, some fish were the sacred animals of certain local districts, where it was forbidden to eat them. The Egyptians were probably the first to regard fishing as a sport as well as a source of food. A sketch has survived which depicts a nobleman fishing from a tank with a rod and line. Harpooning and fowling with a throw stick were also popular sports for the wealthy.

The River Nile was home to a great variety of creatures, from tiny water-snails to

Above: Fishing on the Nile with a draw net, from a Theban tomb painting; c. 1250 B.C.

Left: This stone wall-carving from a very early tomb at Saqqara shows fishermen on the Nile. One of the men rescues a lamb from the water, away from the jaws of a crocodile below.

Right: Papyrus painting showing the harvesting of flax from which linen was made; c. 1350 B.C. (British Museum.)

massive crocodiles. Most were harmless, but a few were dangerous to those using the river. The Nile was also the natural habitat of the hippopotamus and the crocodile. The Egyptians regarded both as very dangerous creatures. As well as hunting for wildfowl in the marshes, and spearing fish from boats, sometimes the villagers went out to kill crocodiles or, less frequently, a hippopotamus. Mummies have been found with bones which seem to have been bitten off by crocodile teeth. Although both animals became associated with gods, the Egyptians hunted the hippopotamus with harpoons. The beautiful temple at Kom Ombo was dedicated to Sobek, the crocodile god, and it is recorded that in 10 B.C. at Lake Moeris, Egyptian priests had a sacred crocodile which they tamed and fed with cakes and honey-wine. Neither the hippopotamus nor the crocodile are to be found in the Egyptian river

Below: Geese from a wall painting at Maidum, c. 2500 B.C.

Left: A statue of a hippopotamus, a creature considered sacred by the Ancient Egyptians – yet hunted by them.

Below: A woman carrying papyrus – the classic flowering plant of Lower Egypt.

nowadays, as they have moved farther south, deep into the Sudan.

PAPYRUS

In the extensive marshy areas of the Nile, the papyrus plant rooted in the mud rose to a great height and spread in dense thickets. The papyrus reed was the raw material of Egyptian paper-making. Papyrus paper was made by cutting thin strips of pith – the spongy tissue in the stem of each reed – and arranging them on a flat stone. The papyrus was then beaten with wooden mallets until natural juice, acting like glue, bound the strips together. The single sheets were pasted into one long roll. The Egyptians are known to have used papyrus as early as the first dynasty (*c.* 3100 B.C.). Papyrus became an expensive government monopoly in later times, and its cultivation was eventually restricted to one particular region. Papyrus no longer grows naturally in Egypt, and much of the thriving tourist trade in paintings claimed to be painted on papyrus is often done on a substitute paper of banana-skin composition.

COMMUNICATION AND TRANSPORT

The Nile formed a perfect artery of communication and, unlike transport by land, it was cheap and quick, since all the cities and towns were easily accessible by boat. Even allowing for all hazards, the Nile is not a particularly formidable river, and nowadays the main leisurely tours of Egypt are on cruiseboats. All the necessary water power is provided by the current and the wind. The current can provide enough power to drift downriver, while the wind blowing from the north can be harnessed to sail upstream.

SAILING SHIPS

The earliest record of a ship under sail is

Right: A modern view of boats on the River Nile. Travel by boat is still the easiest way to reach much of the country, as it was in ancient times. In this photo, you can see the narrow strip of fertile soil close beside the river, where the land is watered by the Nile floods. In the distance, you can see the dry desert and mountains.

Below: Model boat under sail. On the prow a man tests the depth of the water, while the large oar is used for steering. c. 1800 B.C. (British Museum.)

depicted on an Egyptian pot which dates from about 3200 B.C. The Egyptians pioneered the development of river craft, and there were many different types built for various functions. Agricultural produce, troops, cattle, wood, stone, and funeral processions were all carried on the Nile and its canals.

The dockyards could launch ships some 200 feet (70 m) long, made of either native wood or conifers from Lebanon. Complete ships, models, detailed drawings, and a technical vocabulary specifying the various types of boat, with lists of their equipment, have survived. The Ancient Egyptian language itself contains many nautical metaphors, and going south was expressed as "going upstream"

"THE GIFT OF THE NILE"

The Nile also gave the Ancient Egyptians prosperity, as the desert that it runs through provided security and protection from invasion. The contrast between these two geographical features affected the mental attitudes of the people who depended on them. They believed that the Nile was the center of

Left: A ship under full sail, from a Theban tomb painting; c. 2250 B.C.

Below: An elegant model boat from Tutankhamun's tomb.

Bottom: A model of a funeral boat which would have carried the deceased on their final journey on the Nile to their tomb; c. 1900 B.C. (British Museum.)

the world, and the most important highway separating east from west. In the cycle of the Nile flood, they could sense the continuity of life.

By contrast, the desert was considered the home of the dead and a place for burial. Since the sun went down in the west, the desolate desert areas on the west bank were chosen for building their cemeteries. In Egyptian mythology, the Nile was like the River Styx of the Greeks, where the soul was ferried from the east to the west bank. In their creation mythology, the first living matter could be likened to the fresh land deposited after the flood. The Egyptians called their country "the gift of the Nile," and the annual flood was seen as the arrival of the Nile god, Hapy.

If the annual flood of the Nile was too high,

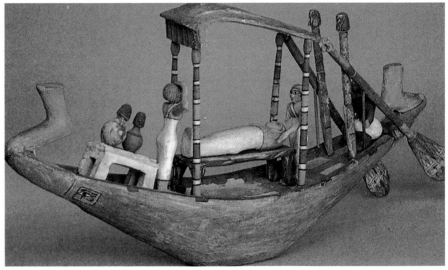

Right: Black granite statue of Hapy, god of the abundant Nile. (British Museum.)

which lasted from about March to August, when the crops could be harvested.

CONTROLLING THE FLOODS

The Egyptians built dikes to prevent the river from flooding the settlements on the mounds which stood out like islands when the Nile flooded the valley. They also laid out a network of reservoirs and canals to contain the water when the flood receded. This was difficult work, and the land had to be reclaimed by leveling the mounds and filling up the depressions in the ground. The water was directed into artificial canals which ran through the provincial settlements. These canals had to be dug and cleared, and the courses planned to irrigate evenly as many fields as possible. The flood-water contained in reservoirs or large, dugout basins was fed into irrigation channels by simple, yet effective, water-raising mechanisms.

The Egyptians built ingenious machines to help them in their work. The introduction of the "shaduf" in the New Kingdom greatly lightened their labor, and is still used in Egypt nowadays. The shaduf consisted of a bucket on a pole, which was lowered into the water and then raised again by a heavy counterweight on the other end of the pole. At the end of the summer, holes were made in the dikes at the highest points, and when the required amount of muddy water had flowed through, the opening was plugged. When the water had been absorbed, work could at last begin and the seed was sown.

THE LABOR FORCE

The building and maintenance of the dikes, reservoirs, and canals went on continuously, and demanded a large labor force which was

the spreading river could destroy the surrounding villages. If it was too low, there was less agricultural land available for food crops. If this low flood was repeated for several consecutive years, famine resulted. The Nile made the Egyptians an agricultural nation from the start, and their need to organize themselves around the river's yearly cycle was crucial to the growth of their civilization. From the earliest times, they managed to determine the seasons of the year by the behavior of the Nile, and developed the first working calendar of 365 days divided into 12 months. They had three seasons, called "akhet", "peret" and "shemu." The season of inundation, akhet began around August, and by November the water had receded enough to plant crops. The final season of shemu represented the drought

Right: The river temple of Philae.

enrolled by a conscription system. In the Old Kingdom, this large, organized labor force could undertake pyramid-building during the inundation season. When there was a political crisis, the maintenance of the system of water supply became disorganized, and in a short time the complete economy of the country would break down. In a land of virtually no rain, irrigation alone made it possible for crops to grow and people to live. In order to help combat the consequences of a poor flood, grain could be stored up against a bad year, or succession of bad years, as in the biblical story of Joseph. The Egyptians also built gauges to measure the rise of the river, and eventually sited these "Nilometers" farther south in order to predict the economic repercussions as early as possible.

The Greek historian, Herodotus, claimed that the first pharaoh, Menes, had the plain of Memphis drained in order to build a new capital there, and thereby altered the course of the Nile. There is also evidence of an immense reservoir constructed in the Faiyum region, 66 square miles (100 sq km) in area,, that had vast dikes and sluices.

THE GREAT DAM

Nowadays, the colossal Aswan High Dam, built between 1960 and 1970, with its own immense reservoir, has ended the traditional annual flood cycle of the River Nile. The immense reservoir, Lake Nasser, created by the dam, submerged whole villages, and has consequently required the resettlement of tens of thousands of people.

Many important ancient remains have been lost, but over 20 monuments were rescued with assistance on an international scale. The most impressive salvage operation was at Abu Simbel, where the vast rock temples were cut into 30-ton blocks, and then reassembled at an identical site above the level of the lake. Similarly, the beautiful temples of Philae were painstakingly transferred stone by stone to a nearby island, safe from the floodwaters of the Nile.

Left: The shaduf enabled farmers to lift water from the river onto their fields with minimum effort. The weight at one end of the pole balanced the bucket at the other.

HIEROGLYPHICS

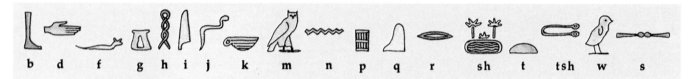

| b | d | f | g | h | i | j | k | m | n | p | q | r | sh | t | tsh | w | s |

The Egyptians were among the earliest people in the world to invent writing, in around 3000 B.C. Most Egyptian buildings, and many works of art, are decorated with inscriptions – lines of picture-writing, called hieroglyphics, carved into their hard-stone surface. Because stone is so tough, and lasts so long, these inscriptions can still be read even after many centuries have passed. Often they are a record of a great achievement, like building a temple or winning a war. The Egyptians hoped that these messages in stone would last forever. We can also learn about the Egyptians from travelers, such as the Greek writer Herodotus, who visited the country around 500 B.C.

When looking at hieroglyphs, we have a natural tendency to view each sign as a representation of a letter, since our written language is dependent upon an alphabet. The idea of an alphabet is something which occurred very late in the history of writing, and the reduction of all the possible sounds and combinations to a written system of some 20 signs took humankind a long time to accomplish.

ANCIENT WRITING

Each hieroglyphic sign does not represent a letter, and does not always represent a word. Beside being pictorial indications of the meaning of words – ideograms – hieroglyphic signs also convey sounds in one, two, or three consonants – phonograms. Writing based solely on picture signs would be impractical, since a complete vocabulary would require thousands of signs. It would be difficult to express clearly and without ambiguity, words for things not easily pictured, and this was probably why signs with a sound value – phonograms – were also necessary. The purely pictorial signs or ideograms could be used at the end of a word to indicate that word's precise meaning – a useful system in the absence of punctuation.

Ancient Egyptian is the second-oldest recorded language. Only Sumerian is believed to be slightly earlier. The first hieroglyphs can be dated to approximately 3100 B.C. (while the latest are almost three-and-a-half-thousand years later, *c.* A.D. 394). It could be claimed that the written language has survived in total for nearly 5000 years, since its final form is still used during Coptic religious services. A small number of Ancient Egyptian words have even found their way into the modern English vocabulary of today, for example, "oasis." Egyptologists have identified five stages in

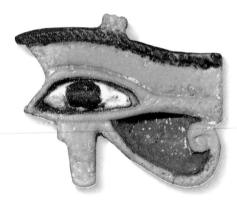

Above: Faience amulet derived from the sacred eye of Horus hieroglyph. (British Museum.)

the development of the language: the Old (*c.* 2650-2135 B.C.), the Middle (*c.* 2135-1785 B.C.), and Late (*c.* 1550-700 B.C.), Demotic (*c.* 700 B.C.-A.D. 500) and, finally, Coptic. This last stage began in the third century A.D., and continued until the Middle Ages when it was replaced by Arabic as the spoken Egyptian language.

Hieroglyphic writing was a highly developed system by which everything, even grammatical forms, could be expressed. Hieroglyphs can be read from right to left, from left to right, and also vertically from top to bottom, according to the composition of the picture. A hieroglyphic inscription was traditionally arranged in columns. Later, it was written in horizontal lines, and the heads of the signs were always turned toward the beginning of the sentence The sequence is continuous, without punctuation marks or spaces to indicate divisions between words.

EGYPTIAN GRAMMAR

Egyptian grammar is completely different from that of European languages and cannot be reduced to a series of simple rules. Mastery of the language takes much concerted study. There are over 6000 documented hieroglyphs covering the whole period during which the scripts were used, although the majority of these was developed for religious reasons in the Greco-Roman period. In general, about 700 were in standard use at any one time.

A striking feature of hieroglyphic writing is its absence of vowels. Egyptologists use the vowels "e" and "a" where necessary, to communicate the language verbally. There are 24 hieroglyphic signs, each representing a consonant, which loosely correspond to the sounds of our modern alphabet. Egyptologists transliterate hieroglyphic sound values into

our modern alphabetic characters to enable pronunciation, but the words would not have sounded the same way in ancient times.

This system of Egyptian alphabetic signs was not generally used for complete words until Greco-Roman times, when various royal names were transcribed into hieroglyphs. It has been claimed that certain hieroglyphs eventually found their way into our own alphabet via Protosinaitic, Phoenician, Greek, and Latin.

Papyrus with a hymn to the god Ra from

Above: The hieratic script in a particularly fine hand from "The Great Harris Papyrus," the longest papyrus known. (British Museum.)

the Book of the Dead. Hieroglyphs came to be used almost exclusively for religious and magical texts. c. 1050 B.C. (British Museum.)

DIVINE WRITING

Hieroglyphs are usually associated with stone inscriptions, and the word itself is actually derived from the Greek *ta hieroglyphica*, meaning "the sacred carved letters." The signs of the script are largely pictorial in character, and the majority of the signs are recognizable pictures of natural or man-made objects. The best examples of the script have an intrinsic beauty of line and color which some claim to be the most beautiful writing ever designed.

It was more than just a writing system, and the Egyptians themselves referred to it as the "writing of the divine words." Like the rep-

resentations in their art, the script was endowed with religious or magical significance. The name of a person inscribed in hieroglyphs was believed to embody his unique identity. If the representation lacked a name, it had no means of continued existence in the afterlife. Therefore, many kings' and gods' names were defaced or erased from monuments by later pharaohs with conflicting ideals. Similarly, existing inscriptions and statues could be taken over and claimed by carving the new royal name on them.

WRITING TEXT

Hieroglyphs were not suitable for writing quickly, and so they were developed into a more stylized, fluent script called Hieratic. This be-

Left: Limestone tablet inscribed with hieroglyphs with a mallet and copper chisels. (British Museum.)

Above: The papyrus of the scribe Ani, one of the finest examples of the Egyptian Book of the Dead. *(British Museum.)*

came the standard administrative and business script, and was also used to record documents of a literary, scientific, and religious nature. It was particularly suitable for writing on papyrus, or fragments of pottery and limestone called ostraca. The text was usually written with a brush or a sharpened reed in black ink, while red ink was sometimes used to highlight special sections. The name Hieratic comes from the Greek *hieratika*, meaning "priestly." This was because, by the Late period, when the Greeks visited Egypt, its use had become confined to religious documents, and Demotic had replaced it as the main "business" script. The name Demotic comes from the Greek *demotika*, meaning "popular," and this refers to its day-to-day writing function. From the Ptolemaic period it was also used for literary compositions, as well as scientific and religious texts.

SCRIBES

Although writing played an important part in Ancient Egyptian society, it is unlikely that literacy can have been widespread among the population. The production of writing and direct access to it was confined to an educated elite, consisting of royalty, state officials, and scribes. The professional scribe was a central figure in every aspect of the country's administration – civil, military, and religious. When an illiterate person needed a document to be read or written he would need to pay for the services of a scribe. It traditionally took a scribe some 12 years to learn and write the 700 or so hieroglyphs in common use by the New Kingdom, and study started at the age of four. Many ancient school exercises have survived – complete with the teacher's corrections – and these were often copies of Egyptian classics in the Hieratic text.

PAPYRUS

Egyptian scribes wrote on paper called papyrus that was made from reeds. The tall papyrus reeds were chopped into short lengths and then peeled. The inner pith was sliced into thin strips. The strips were arranged in layers on a wooden board. They overlapped in a criss-cross pattern. They were then covered with a cloth and pounded with a heavy mallet. This made them stick together into a single sheet. The cloth was removed and the newly made sheet of papyrus was polished with a smooth stone. It could then be trimmed. The scribes used ink made of soot. Sometimes they decorated their writings with red ink too.

Scribes had to combine several hieroglyphs to "spell" each word in the documents they were writing. Hieroglyphs could be written across or down the page, and words were "spelled" without vowels. Scribes also kept records of tribute payments. Tribute – paid in food, treasures, or by sending men to work – was collected by the pharaoh's officials from ordinary people.

COPTIC SCRIPT

In Egypt's Roman and Christian period, the Coptic script developed as the other native scripts declined. The word "copt" is derived from the Arabic *gubti*, a corruption of the Greek word for Egypt. It was used by the Arabs in the seventh century to denote the native inhabitants of the country. Coptic consists of 24 letters of the Greek alphabet, combined with six Demotic characters.

The development of this standard form of the alphabet, which was well established by the fourth century A.D., is closely associated with the spread of Christianity in Egypt. In its earliest form, Coptic was used to write native magical texts, and it was not initially devised for translating the Gospels. Since it is still spoken in Coptic religious services some people believe it could reveal clues to the pronunciation of the original Ancient Egyptian language, although the links may have become too distant with the passage of time.

THE ROSETTA STONE

The art of reading hieroglyphs was lost for centuries and it was a Frenchman called Jean-François Champollion (1790-1832) who became the first to decipher them in full. The most important key to this forgotten writing was the famous Rosetta Stone, discovered in

Above: The Rosetta Stone consists of three scripts – hieroglyphs at the top, Demotic in the middle, and Greek at the bottom. It is a decree by all the priests of Egypt in favor of the reigning king, Ptolomy V.

1799, which had a bilingual text.

This was a decree of the Pharaoh Ptolemy V written in Ancient Greek – a known language – and two Ancient Egyptian scripts, Demotic and hieroglyphic. Comparing these scripts, and making use of his excellent knowledge of Coptic, Champollion studied copies of other hieroglyphic inscriptions. After considerable research, he was able to recognize not only some of the letters of the hieroglyphic alphabet, but also a range of other hieroglyphs from royal cartouches. He managed to decipher 79 different royal names, of which he recognized and tabulated all the letters one by one. Then, using the "alphabet," all the letters of which he had progressively recovered, he managed to identify words. In only a couple of years he managed to compile a dictionary and grammar.

Although the readings of kings' names provided the key to the writing system, it would not have led to an understanding of the Egyptian language without the assistance of Coptic. In studying the Rosetta Stone text, Champollion's knowledge of Coptic enabled him to work out the phonetic values of particular hieroglyphic signs, while his understanding of the Greek text helped him to identify the pictorial characters.

With a knowledge of the language, we are now able to translate the countless ancient writings that have survived. The wisdom texts were the most highly regarded and oldest writings, and were popular throughout Egyptian history. They often contain moral codes and represent a high level of thinking. Beside religious literature and business records, the Ancient Egyptian writings include subjects as varied as poetry, medicine and mathematics.

Below: Painted hieroglyphs on a Middle Kingdom coffin. (British Museum.)

THE
LEGACY OF ANCIENT
EGYPT

The impressive monuments and fascinating artifacts are today's visible evidence of Egypt's past glory. However, many invisible aspects of our modern civilization have their origins in Ancient Egypt. The Egyptians' ideas spread to Europe via the Greeks and the Romans, who were impressed by the achievements of a civilization so much older than their own, and whose own cultures drew heavily on this legacy. Ancient Egypt has become increasingly distant, mysterious, and fascinating ever since. It has also become a potent vehicle for escapism, which has inspired art, novels, crime fiction, science fiction, epic and horror movies. In addition, many people develop a quest to discover some hidden or secret knowledge in Ancient Egypt, and devise complex theories on the construction and purpose of the pyramids. The Ancient Egyptians themselves never went out of their way to spread their culture and religion to the rest of the world, and their influence took place by force of circumstance.

Trade helped to spread Egyptian culture throughout the ancient world. The Egyptians needed wood, metals, and semiprecious stones, while their monopoly on African products, particularly gold, attracted countless foreigners. Ideas and technical knowledge traveled with produce. Cultural interchange between Africa, Asia, and the Mediterranean countries increased during certain periods of invasion and conquest. The Phoenicians, who were sea-faring traders, borrowed and adapted many Egyptian architectural and artistic elements and spread them throughout the Mediterranean to mainland Greece.

The early Greek writers who traveled to Egypt themselves acknowledged the influence

Below: Israel in Egypt, *by Sir Edward Poynter (1836-1919).*

of Egypt on Greek principles of architecture and geometry. The earliest, archaic Greek sculptures reflect both the pose – with the left foot forward – and the proportions of those of Egypt. Before Socrates, followers of Pythagoras came to Egypt to complete their studies of geometry, astronomy, and theology, and Egyptian story-telling was also an important influence on the development of the Hellenistic novel. In addition, some aspects of Ancient Greek religion can be traced to Egypt. The Greeks were also inspired by Egyptian medical science, and Egyptian doctors were employed by the Hittites and the Persians.

Scholars have attempted to demonstrate the development of our own alphabet from hieroglyphic signs, and certain concepts of Egyptian law may also have come down to us. However, perhaps the greatest Ancient Egyptian legacy has been its calendar, which was adopted by the Romans and forms the basis of our own Gregorian calendar.

ROMAN CULTURE

The Romans, like the Greeks before them, absorbed many native religious beliefs after they conquered Egypt. They adopted Egyptian burial practices, developing a sophisticated embalming technique and style of funerary portraiture. Many Egyptian gods were also worshiped, although their true nature was often totally misunderstood. The Romans imported many Egyptian statues, and made many, often spurious, copies of them. Obelisks stood in the Temple of Isis and in the

Right: A Greek-period bronze statuette of the god Amen Ra shows how Egyptian forms were misrepresented by later cultures. (British Museum.)

circuses in Rome. Since Rome became the most important city in the classical and Christian world, the Roman selection and interpretation of Egyptian forms strongly influenced the way the rest of Europe viewed Ancient Egypt. Consequently, the knowledge handed down to medieval and Renaissance Europe was largely governed by what interested classical and Byzantine scholars.

CHRISTIAN CULTURE

The Bible has provided the only point of access to Ancient Egypt for many Christians over the centuries, and it is inevitably colored by certain prejudices. The Old Testament gives a general impression of the Egyptians as a powerful pagan state oppressing a weaker and devout nomadic people.

The Jews, like many nomadic people, were attracted to Egypt's land of plenty, and when they left, they must have taken with them many native Egyptian ideas. Egyptian hymns and wisdom literature were known in Canaan from the time of the New Kingdom, and they influenced certain Old Testament writings. Meanwhile, Solomon may well have been inspired by the efficiency of the Egyptian bureaucracy when organizing the Jewish kingdom.

It is often demonstrated that the Christian religion contains many practices and images

Above: Bronze figure of the god Horus as a Roman soldier. The Romans adapted many Egyptian gods into their own culture, without fully understanding their original religious function. (British Museum.)

Right: Mummy of a Roman boy. The Romans adopted the native Egyptian burial customs and added naturalistic portraits to them. (British Museum.)

which had their roots in pagan Egypt. This is quite understandable since, during the formative years of Christianity, the religious rituals inherited from the Romans were already steeped in Egyptian traditions. When the powerful Roman Empire officially adopted the new Christian religion, it embraced many existing concepts and images. In particular, the cult of Isis, so strong in the early Roman Empire, could have provided a prototype image of the Virgin and Child through the many representations of Isis suckling Horus. It is recorded that an ancient statue of Isis survived in a French church until the sixteenth century, while, in a different French church, the birth of Isis continues to be celebrated nowadays.

LINK TO CHRISTIANITY

The popular representation of Christ triumphant over harmful beasts bears a striking resemblance to the image of Horus triumphant over the crocodile. Many similar parallels can be drawn between the portrayal of certain Christian saints and Egyptian gods, while holy attributes like the halo, crook, and the idea of winged men and women as angels have Egyptian precedents.

The central Christian emblem, the cross, is often represented on early Coptic monuments as the Egyptian ankh sign of life, and is still clearly present on medieval tombstones in the Balkans. Many subconscious Egyptian elements would have been conveyed by the bishops from Egypt, who were highly influential at the early church councils in Rome.

Egyptian literature also influenced many famous Eastern folklore tales, like Sinbad and Ali Baba, while many ancient phrases and sayings probably survive in modern Egypt and

Left: Painted fresco in a Coptic church. The early Christian Church in Egypt borrowed many elements from the ancient "pagan" heritage, and the Ancient Egyptian language is still spoken today during services.

the rest of Africa. Certain Ancient Egyptian techniques and ritual practices have survived among the central African peoples, probably via the later Ethiopian kingdom of Meroe. In modern Egypt, although the influence of the Islamic culture has been considerable, many age-old customs have survived.

In the countryside, the shaduf is still used to water the fields, as depicted in ancient times, and many aspects of village life have change little. Some boundaries have hardly altered, and certain ancient place names have remained virtually the same. At Luxor, a sacred bark is carried in honor of an Islamic saint, very much as it would have been for the god Amun in ancient times.

Many superstitions have also survived, such as leaving food or burning incense for dead

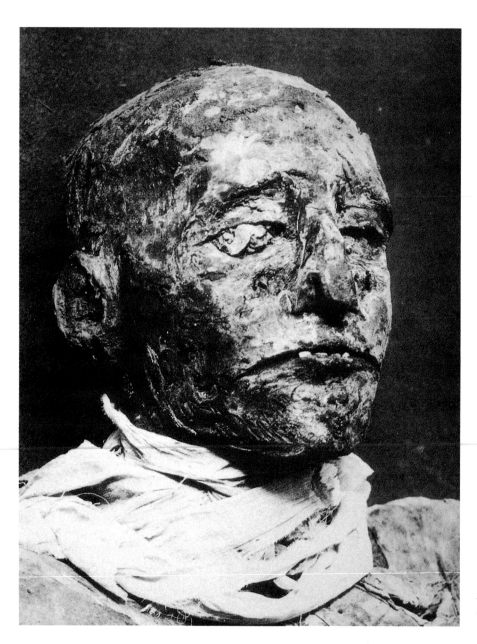

Left: The well-preserved mummy of Ramses III, which has provided the model for many horror movies.

Left: The Finding of Moses, *by Sir Lawrence Alma Tadema (1836-1912). Biblical subjects provided artists with an excuse for indulging in fanciful visions of Ancient Egypt.*

relatives. There is also a fear of the "evil eye," and charms are still kept as protection against evil.

MYSTICAL INFLUENCE

Ancient Egypt has continued to be a source of inspiration for mystics and followers of the occult. The Hermetic creed, alchemy, and astrology probably originated from Alexandria, which became a major cultural and trading center in the ancient world. It was here that many Ancient Egyptian, Greek, and Near Eastern ideas and beliefs merged together. Hermetic writings popularized the notion that Egyptians possessed true wisdom.

Although astrology arrived late in Egyptian history, probably from Western Asia, there are many depictions of stars, constellations, and maps of the sky which have been mistaken for true zodiacs by mystics. The Egyptians did have a system of determining lucky and unlucky influences on the day, as in modern daily horoscopes, which, however, had no connection with the 12 signs of the zodiac. The lucky or unlucky character of the day was derived from mythological events which had taken place on these particular days. In Egyptian literature, there was also a belief that certain numbers had a magical significance. This may have found its way into modern superstition for unlucky numbers.

The earliest tale about a magician is in the Westcar papyrus, which dates from *c.* 1700 B.C., and many psychics, fortune-tellers and palmists call themselves by Egyptian names or claim to be reincarnated Egyptian priests or priestesses. The animal-headed gods, mysterious hieroglyphic writing, sacred amulets, and funerary beliefs of the Ancient Egyptians provide subject matter for clairvoyants and psychic writers. It is even rumored that they sell genuine powdered mummy in a New York

Above: Sandstorm in the Desert, *by David Roberts (1796-1864), who visited Egypt in 1839. He sketched many monuments, and his drawings were published in a famous series of lithographs.*

pharmacy for use in occult magic potions.

THE CURSE OF THE MUMMY

The Ancient Egyptian influence on the occult is reinforced by the many tales of the "mummy's curse" which continue to capture public imagination. The earliest record of a ghost story involving a mummy was written in France in 1699. The mummy, together with

Dracula and Frankenstein, prove that the theme has remained ever-popular for horror movies. Ancient Egypt's connection with the occult was publicized when the so-called "Curse of Tutankhamun" was claimed by the press to be responsible for the death of Lord Carnarvon. Carnarvon, the expedition's sponsor who had a history of ill-health, died from an infected mosquito bite shortly after the tomb's

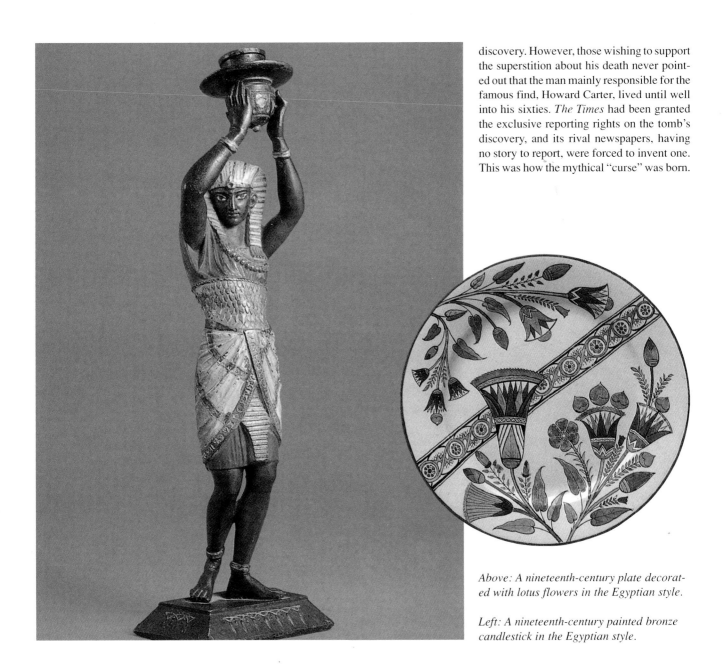

discovery. However, those wishing to support the superstition about his death never pointed out that the man mainly responsible for the famous find, Howard Carter, lived until well into his sixties. *The Times* had been granted the exclusive reporting rights on the tomb's discovery, and its rival newspapers, having no story to report, were forced to invent one. This was how the mythical "curse" was born.

Above: A nineteenth-century plate decorated with lotus flowers in the Egyptian style.

Left: A nineteenth-century painted bronze candlestick in the Egyptian style.

Right: The Egyptian House, Penzance, England. Built in the 1930s, this structure represents the Egyptian Revival style in architecture.

Left: A colossal bas-relief from a modern hardware center in Kensington, London, England, which reflects the vogue for Egyptian Revival architecture during the 1990s.

Above: A silver salt dish, c. 1840s, decorated in the Egyptian Revival style.

INFLUENCE ON ART

In addition to influencing the occult sciences, Ancient Egypt has continued to inspire Western art through its exotic and romantic associations. In the nineteenth century, a number of European painters succeeded in producing some highly imaginative reconstructions of Ancient Egypt. This was in response to a general taste for Middle Eastern subjects at the time, and many artists traveled all over the Islamic world. The subject matter of their paintings inevitably included turbaned Arabs, bustling bazaars, camels, palm trees, and mildly pornographic harem scenes.

The pyramids and the ancient ruins of Egypt were part of this romantic ideal, and are often depicted in exaggerated perspective with dramatic sunsets. These elements of the fantastic, exotic, and erotic were part of many artists' fanciful visions of Ancient Egypt. Their remarkable attention to detail was a reflection of contemporary Orientalist and Pre-Raphaelite ideals. Many artists must have visited museums in order to make accurate studies of original ancient artifacts. The Bible also provided Ancient Egyptian themes for paintings which are frequently charged with considerable sentiment and melodrama. Many of these images became popularized through engravings in contemporary family Bibles and children's scripture books.

THE DECORATIVE ARTS

For the decorative arts and architecture, Ancient Egyptian motifs provided a variation on the highly fashionable neo-classical style. This is often called the "Egyptian Revival," and it was popular in France and England throughout the Napoleonic Wars, with their Egyptian connection.

However, the Egyptian elements were

Left: This sphinx car mascot from a 1920s' car reflects the popularity of Egyptian motifs following the discovery of Tutankhamun's tomb.

stylized to suit contemporary tastes, and the figures took on a rounder, plumper style, reminiscent of the Ancient Greco-Roman Egyptian style. "Egyptianizing" was also a feature of English and French furniture of the Regency and Empire periods, and was applied to other items like clocks, candelabra and porcelain. This mixture of Egyptian and classical forms was also used in buildings as varied as mills, law courts, Masonic lodges, and cemeteries. By the 1850s, the inclusion of an Egyptian court in the Great Exhibition in London showed that Ancient Egypt had captured the British public imagination, reflecting the Victorian taste for ornament and decoration.

In the twentieth century, the artistic interpretation of Ancient Egypt has become less cluttered and elaborate and more "modern." The lofty, spacious, and geometric character of Egyptian forms are more in tune with modern taste than the classical style. The discovery of Tutankhamun's tomb in the 1920s was a major influence on a new design movement called Art Deco. Many Egyptian forms were stylized and incorporated into contemporary architecture, furniture, sculpture, and graphic art. Ancient Egypt also had a big influence on the newly formed movie industry, which was generated from Hollywood. The design of many cinema façades was inspired by Egyptian temple architecture, and helped to enhance the whole fantasy world of movies. Meanwhile, Ancient Egyptian themes provided the perfect vehicle for escapist epics like *Land of the Pharaohs, The Ten Commandments,* and *Cleopatra*, which had huge sets with casts of thousands. This grand vision of Egypt's ancient splendor is similarly captured in the world of opera by Verdi's spectacular *Aïda*.

ANCIENT EGYPT AND MODERN ART
Modern artists continue to be inspired by Ancient Egypt, and highly original talents like Pablo Picasso and Henry Moore both acknowledged its influence on their formative work. In recent years, architects have taken a renewed interest in Egypt, and forms such as the pyramid continue to be stylishly applied to many public and commercial buildings. The Egyptian style is so ancient that it appears modern, and as we progress into the future, so our knowledge of civilized humans' most distant past become more relevant.

Left: Verdi's epic opera Aïda *continues to be staged as a lavish spectacle and perpetuates the myth of Egypt's ancient splendour.*

A COMPARATIVE CHRONOLOGY OF ANCIENT EGYPT

DATE	IN EGYPT	PERIOD	ELSEWHERE IN THE WORLD
500 A.D.	Last-known Demotic inscription Last hieroglyphic inscription Queen Zenobia of Palmyra occupies Egypt Bucolic War Alexandrian riots Death of Cleopatra	GRECO- ROMAN PERIOD	Classical Mayan culture of Middle America Rome sacked Constantinople founded Middle Moche culture in South America Main building begins at Teotihuacan Jewish Diaspora Vesuvius engulfs Pompeii Claudian invasion of Britain
0	Temple built at Edfu Rebel native rulers at Thebes Ptolemy Lagos rules as pharaoh Alexander the Great in Egypt Last native pharaohs	PTOLEMAIC PERIOD DYNASTY 21-30 LATE DYNASTIC PERIOD	Birth of Christ Buddhism reaches China Julius Caesar invades Britain Destruction of Carthage Hannibal crosses Alps Start of unified Chinese Empire Death of Emperor Ashoka Alexander the Great in India Construction of Parthenon Defeat of Persians at Marathon
500 B.C.	Persians annex Egypt Greek colonies in Egypt Assyrian invasions Kushite kings rule Egypt Sheshonq I sacks Jerusalem Greatest power of Theban high priests		Birth of Buddha Nebuchadnezzar destroys Jerusalem Medes destroy Babylon Rise of cities in India Beginnings of Great Wall of China Rome founded First Olympic Games held Death of Solomon David rules from Jerusalem Chavin culture of South America
1000 B.C.	Extensive tomb-robbing at Thebes Ramses III repulses sea peoples Merneptah checks Libyan invasions Clashes with Hittites in Syria	DYNASTY 18-20, NEW KINGDOM	Fall of Troy Olmec culture of Middle America Main building phase at Stonehenge

A COMPARATIVE CHRONOLOGY OF ANCIENT EGYPT

DATE	IN EGYPT	PERIOD	ELSEWHERE IN THE WORLD
	Tutankhamun returns to Thebes Akhenaten founds Akhenaten Luxor temple begun Tuthmosis III conquers Syria Queen Hatshepsut rules as pharaoh		Shang dynasty in China Fall of Knossos and Minoan Empire
1500 B.C.	First tomb in Valley of Kings Amosis expels Hyksos Thebans oppose Hyksos Hyksos seize Memphis Avaris becomes Hyksos capital Trade with Asia, Africa, and Mediterranean islands Karnak temple begun Fortresses built in Nubia New capital at Itj-tawy Mentuhotpe II reunites Egypt	DYNASTY 13-17, SECOND INTERMEDIATE PERIOD DYNASTY 11-12, MIDDLE KINGDOM	Hammurabi codifies law
2000 B.C.	Civil war between Thebes and Heracleopolis Pepi II reigns 94 years Unas pyramid first to contain text Sun temples at Abu Gurab Expeditions to Punt (Somalia)	DYNASTY 7-10, FIRST INTERMEDIATE PERIOD DYNASTY 3-6, OLD KINGDOM	First pottery made in Middle America Earliest smelting of iron in Middle East Indo-Europeans enter Anatolia Sargon of Agade Indus Valley cultures of India Tablet archives at Ebla
2500 B.C.	Khufu builds Great Pyramid First true pyramid at Dahshur Step pyramid at Saqqara Expeditions to Sinai and Nubia Trade with Asia and tropical Africa First stone architectural elements	DYNASTY 1-2, ARCHAIC PERIOD	Royal burials at Ur

A COMPARATIVE CHRONOLOGY OF ANCIENT EGYPT

DATE	IN EGYPT	PERIOD	ELSEWHERE IN THE WORLD
3000 B.C.	Invention of hieroglyphic writing Egypt united, Memphis founded Glazed composition made for first time Hard-stone vessels produced Painted buff pottery	PREDYNASTIC PERIOD NAQADA II CULTURE	First pottery made in South America Sumerians introduce writing
3500 B.C.	Stone vessels first produced White-paint incised pottery First models of human figure Metal-working practised Blacked-topped red pottery first produced	NAQADA I CULTURE BADARIAN CULTURE	
4000 B.C.	Cereals and flax grown	EGYPTIAN STONE AGE	